I0489811

MICRO HABITS IN 15 MINUTES

**An Easy Way to Build Good Habits
and Replace Bad Ones**

by Ivan Kuznietsov

COPYRIGHT AND DISCLAIMERS

Micro Habits in 15 Minutes by Ivan Kuznietsov

The author reserves the right to make any changes he deems necessary to future versions of the publication to ensure its accuracy.

ABOUT THE AUTHOR

Ivan Kuznietsov is a certified Agile Coach and international author focused on habits and continuous improvement. He is known for delivering highly actionable, world-class behavior change strategies for teams and individuals. Ivan writes books with one simple aim in mind: to teach people new micro habits in 15 minutes a day.

Ivan was born in Ukraine, but currently he lives and works in Vienna, Austria.

DEDICATION

To my family who supports me to explore.

EPIGRAPH

micro

> • extremely small in scale or scope

habit

> • a routine or practice performed regularly

PREFACE

I had experimented with personal development strategies for a decade. When I accidentally started my first micro habit in 2018—and the changes I made were actually lasting—I realized the prior techniques I relied on were complete failures. But the truth is the problem wasn't with them, it was with my approach to them.

The science in Micro Habits book series exposes the most popular personal growth strategies as predictably inconsistent and shows why micro habits are the most effective and reliable way to live a happy and productive life.

When you start reading Micro Habits, and then again after you start your first micro habit, you'll wonder why nobody told you about this strategy before, and where it's been all your life. Well, nobody told me either. But let's focus on your bright future because micro habits will surprisingly change your life.

ABOUT MICRO HABITS BOOK SERIES

Micro Habits can change your life in 15 minutes a day!

Dreaming big is important, but often, big goals start with micro-steps. Bite-size, low-time-commitment habits can help you gradually achieve your goals in doable steps. Just a few minutes a day can lay the foundation you need to make your big dreams come true.

What are Micro Habits?

Micro habits are tiny, everyday habits that steer you toward big results. Because they are too small and not time-consuming, they are easy to incorporate into your daily life. If you've ever made New Year's resolutions, you know how hard they can be to see through. But micro habits aren't daunting—rather, they're quick wins to keep you motivated.

Here are a few ways micro shifts lead to lasting change:

- Micro habits can help to break bad habits.
- Tiny life changes make it easier to implement new, productive habits.
- The adjustments feel natural over time and eventually become a normal part of your character and routine.

Micro habits are easy, small changes that lead to big shifts in your health, finances, and personal growth. If you are ready to improve your life, in the Micro Habits book series you will find the most useful micro habits to try, whether your goals are to get fit, be more creative, or just improve the quality of your life. Get started on micro habits today and notice how they keep you motivated over time.

ABOUT MICRO HABITS IN 15 MINUTES BOOK

New Habit in One Sitting

"Micro Habits was a great read. I learned a lot and think it'll be helpful to a lot of people." —Jeff Beck, Goodreads user

No matter your goals, Micro Habits offers a proven formula for improving day by day. Ivan, a certified Agile Coach, reveals practical strategies that will teach you exactly how to form good habits, break bad ones, and master the micro behaviors that lead to remarkable results.

Learn how to:

- overcome a lack of willpower and

motivation;
- make time for new habits;
- change your behavior to make success easier;
- get back on track when you fall off course;
- ...and much more.

Whether you are a team looking to win a championship, or simply an individual who wishes to get yourself in a better shape or achieve any other goal, Micro Habits will reshape the way you think about goals and progress, and give you the strategy you need to transform your habits.

CONTENTS

ROME WASN'T BUILT IN A DAY, BUT THEY WERE LAYING BRICKS EVERY DAY

"Rome wasn't built in a day"

People use the phrase "Rome wasn't built in a day" to remind someone of the time needed to create something significant.

And it's true. It takes time — sometimes months or even years — to master a skill, craft, or habit. And while it's good to keep perspective on your big dreams, I think it's better to remember the other side of this story:

Rome wasn't built in a day, but they were laying bricks every hour.

The problem is that it can be really easy to overestimate the importance of building your Roman empire and underestimate the importance of laying another brick.

But it's just another brick. Why think about it? Much better to worry about the dream of Rome. Right?

Actually, Rome is just the result — the bricks are the system. The system is greater than the goal. Focusing on your habits is more important than worrying about your outcomes.

Of course, there's nothing necessarily impressive about laying a brick. It's not a fantastic amount of work. It's not a grand feat of strength or stamina or intelligence. Nobody is going to applaud you for it.

But laying a brick every day, year after year — that's how you build an empire. You can start small. You can focus on improving by 1% each day. You can simply lay brick by brick.

You don't have to build everything you want today, but you do have to find a way to lay another brick right now. If you want more practical ideas for how to build new habits (and break bad ones), continue to read the Micro Habits book series, which will show you how micro changes in habits can lead to remarkable results.

Brick by brick.

* * *

WHAT ARE HABITS?

"Motivation is what gets you started. Habit is what keeps you going," Jim Ryun

Let's define habits first. Habits are the small decisions you make and actions you perform every day. According to researchers at Duke University, habits account for about 40 percent of our behaviors on any given day.

Your life today is essentially the sum of your habits:

How strong or weak you are? — A result of your habits.

How successful or unsuccessful you are? — A result of your habits.

How happy or unhappy you are? — A result of your habits.

What you repeatedly do (i.e. what you spend time thinking about and doing each day) ultimately forms the person you are, the things you believe, and the personality that you portray. Everything I write about — from focus and productivity to exercises and nutrition — starts with better habits. In short, when you learn to transform your habits, you can transform your life.

* * *

WHAT ARE MICRO HABITS?

"Doing a micro action is infinitely bigger than procrastinating," Ivan

Micro habits are very small positive behavior that you force yourself to do every day. Its "too small to fail" nature makes it weightless, deceptively powerful, and a superior habit-building strategy. You will have no choice but to believe in yourself when you're always moving forward. The barrier to the first step is so low that even depressed or "stuck" people can find early success and begin to reverse their lives right away.

* * *

WHAT IS THE DIFFERENCE BETWEEN MICRO HABITS AND ATOMIC HABITS?

Let's start with *Atomic Habits*, the book written by James Clear. No matter your goals, Atomic Habits offers a proven framework for improving — day by day. Atomic Habits will reshape the way you think about progress and success, and give you the tools and strategies you need to transform your habits — whether you are a team looking to win a championship, an organization hoping to redefine an industry, or simply an individual who wishes to lose weight, quit smoking, reduce stress or achieve any other goal. Speaking generally, Atomic Habits are all about *"motivation."*

Now let's figure out what *Micro Habits* book is about. Micro Habits are all about *"action."* When it comes to change, micro is mighty. For example, start with one pushup a day, not a one-hour workout; or one deep breath each morning rather than an hour of meditation. The action here is the most crucial point.

* * *

WHY DO MICRO HABITS WORK?

Micro habits use a tiny amount of your willpower to "spark" you to action every day. This spark will lead to further action beyond your initial small requirement. Scientific studies on willpower show it's limited, and motivation is erratic because it's feelings-based, so by using willpower in the most "cost-efficient" way, we can guarantee progress that builds and builds into something special.

* * *

WHAT MICRO HABITS WILL DO FOR YOU?

Micro Habits will allow you to incorporate new healthy behaviors into your life without the procrastination, guilt, and repeated failure associated with other strategies such as "setting goals" or even "dreaming big." The basis of what makes the Micro Habits strategy so powerful is it naturally creates a *positive encouragement spiral*. When you succeed every day, your general motivation level increases and you'll begin to believe in yourself. More commonly, people are trapped in negative downward spirals, because when they feel bad, they don't want to take action, which makes them feel even worse about themselves.

Micro Habits reverses these downward spirals by shifting momentum positively and continuing it every day, break by break. Once you do something for 30, 60, or 90 days, your brain will begin to form it into a habit, and you will have no choice but to believe in yourself. The barrier to the first step is so low that even "stuck" people can find early success and begin to reverse their lives right away.

All books in the *Micro Habits* book series will explore exactly how and why micro habits work in different areas of life, as well as give you critical implementation tips.

Your mindset plays a key role in building habits successfully. That's why Micro Habits books will tell you what mindsets can sabotage you, what mindsets ensure success, and how your brain will react to the changes you're making at every step. It's important to know what's going on so that you can react appropriately to challenges that will arise. My goal is to guide you on this path.

* * *

THREE STAGES OF BUILDING MICRO HABITS

"Success is a few simple disciplines, practiced every day while failure is simply a few errors in judgment, repeated every day," Jim Rohn

In *Micro Habits,* I bring my experience coaching people to help you achieve any goal of your choice. You just need to understand the simple formula that will make Micro Habits work for you:

Start with a micro-action right now. Repeat it daily. Let it grow with time.

Whenever you come home, take a sit-up once.

Smile whenever you look in the mirror.

Whenever you get in bed, turn off the wi-fi.

Repeat.

Change can be easy — once it starts, it grows. I will show you exactly how. In the next few chapters, we will focus on the theory of habit building, and after that, we will focus on practicing.

* * *

THE 1ST STAGE — START WITH A MICRO-ACTION RIGHT NOW

Wherever you are, start to build your habit right now. Dreaming about being in good shape? Put the book aside (don't worry, I will wait) and start with one push-up and one sit-up.

... I am still waiting...

So, how it was? I bet you feel a little bit better than a few seconds ago. Your brain starts producing dopamine because you realize you are one step closer to your goal.

Whatever you want to achieve, always start with a micro-action. It's nice to dream big, but it is more important to act small.

* * *

THE 2ND STAGE — REPEAT IT DAILY

Once you started to build your micro habit, it is very important to be consistent. Repeat regularly what you already started. Have you started reading 5 pages a day of your favorite book? Repeat it daily.

It looks like 5 pages are not significant, but multiply it by 365 days and you will have 1825 pages. It's a few good books — much more than most people read per year.

Remember:

The goal is not so important as a trajectory you move on.

I can explain:

To read 10 books per year is a goal.

Reading 5 pages per day is a trajectory you move on.

Being consistent on your trajectory will make you happy no matter whether achieve you your goals or not.

* * *

THE 3RD STAGE — LET IT GROW WITH TIME

This is the easiest stage. No effort is required. Let your micro habit grow by itself. It just needs time. It will happen automatically.

Do you feel ready to add one additional push-up to your exercises? — Add it!

Want to read 5 pages more? — Read it!

No pressure, just inspiration. Suddenly you will realize that your micro habits are growing without your efforts. Micro habits become your routine and part of your life. So let it be.

* * *

THREE STEPS TO UNDERSTAND AND HACK YOUR HABITS

"You have power over your mind — not outside events. Realize this, and you will find strength," Marcus Aurelius

Admit it: You've got a few pesky habits you'd like to kick. Oh, and I know you've got big plans for how you're going to change your life. But how long have you been saying this without actually springing into action?

I suspect the reason you haven't changed much (despite wanting to), is that you're going about your habit replacement all wrong. Now, let me introduce a new framework for looking at your habits from a microscopic perspective in order to hack them to be your best choices.

* * *

STEP 1 —
CHANGE YOUR
IDENTITY

Sometimes it's hard to admit we're on a bad path, even to ourselves. The more that you identify with a particular behavior you link it to the idea that "This is who I am." When you associate yourself with the type of person who does this habit, it becomes more difficult to filter your actions. The behavior is tied up in your identity.

For example when you say to yourself, "I'm the type of person who reads every day," you are adopting the identity of this habit. In this sense, it's not even really a behavior change to regularly read. It's essentially you acting in alignment with the person you already believe you are.

That's why micro habits are so meaningful. If you do five sit-ups, on its own the behavior, it doesn't count for much. But long term, you're casting a vote for the person you want to be. And that's meaningful. So even if the habit is very small, it is reinforcing your desired identity.

* * *

STEP 2 — CHANGE YOUR BEHAVIOR

Think about it this way: Every behavior produces multiple outcomes across time. Let's take something like eating a cake. If you eat a cake right now, the immediate outcome is favorable — it's tasty and sugary. But if you continue that habit over say, multiple months, the ultimate outcome is unfavorable — your cholesterol levels increase, you probably gain weight, etc.

But then you take a good habit, let's say exercising. The immediate outcome of exercising is unfavorable — you sweat and your muscles ache. However, the ultimate outcome is favorable — you lose weight, you gain muscle, you feel better, etc.

Often, we make decisions based on the immediate outcome, rather than the ultimate outcome. A lot of the challenge of addressing bad habits and harnessing good ones has to do with pulling the consequences of your bad habits into the present moment, so you feel a little bit of that pain instantaneously. At the same time, you need to pull the long-term rewards of your good habits into the present moment, to make them more immediately satisfying.

* * *

STEP 3 —
CHANGE YOUR
ENVIRONMENT

Relying solely on self-control is a recipe for failure. All habits, when formed, are linked to some kind of context. Certain contexts in your life repeat themselves again and again. So the more you face a particular context, the more you face problems that are associated with that particular context. Soon your brain starts to link certain solutions to certain problems, which is to say it starts to associate certain habits with certain contexts.

For example, you put your sneakers on and they're untied. So there's a problem that needs to be solved — you need to get your shoe tied.

The first time you ever tie your sneakers, it's sort of

arduous and it takes a while. But after you tie your shoe 10, 100, or 1000 times, pretty soon your brain has just automated that habit, which is to say it has automated the solution to the problem that you face repeatedly.

Pretty soon the context of looking down at an untied shoe means you don't even think about it, you just automatically get into the shoe-tying mode.

That's true for pretty much every habit. If someone walks into their house after work and glances at their sofa, for one person that might be the place where they play computer games for an hour every evening, and for another, that same context might be where they read for an hour every night.

The point here is the context is tied to the habit. Pretty much all of your environments, or contexts, already have habits and associations that are tied to them. So to build a new habit in the same context requires you to overpower those associations.

Here are a few ways you can redesign your environment and make the triggers for your preferred habits more obvious:

- If you want to remember to take your medication each morning, put your pill bottle near your bed or directly next to the faucet on the bathroom counter.
- If you want to read more frequently, place your book on your working table.
- If you want to drink more water, fill up a water bottle each morning and place it on the kitchen table, so you will see it each time before sitting to eat.

If you want to make a habit a big part of your life, make the trigger for this habit a big part of your environment.

* * *

DON'T ELIMINATE BAD HABITS — REPLACE THEM WITH GOOD ONES

"Waste no more time arguing about what a good man should be. Be one," Marcus Aurelius

Bad habits can interrupt your life and prevent you from accomplishing your goals. They jeopardize your health — both physically and mentally. And they waste your energy and time.

So why do you still do them? And most importantly, is there anything you can do about it?

Let's put it the next way. When we want to make our homes more comfortable and attractive, we replace old furniture with new ones. We don't want to through away old furniture months before buying new ones because we don't want to live in empty rooms, right? The same goes for habits.

It's better not to eliminate bad habits, but replace them with better ones.

Now let's focus on the practice of making changes in the real world. How can you replace your bad habits with good ones? Well, let's look at the roots of your bad habits first, because you can solve the problem only when you recognize it.

* * *

WHAT CAUSES BAD HABITS?

Most of your bad habits are caused by two things…

Stress and boredom.

Most of the time, bad habits are simply a way of dealing with stress and boredom. Everything from biting your nails to overspending on a shopping spree to drinking every weekend to wasting time on the internet can be a simple response to stress and boredom.

But it doesn't have to be that way. You can teach yourself new and healthy ways to deal with stress and boredom, which you can then substitute in place of your bad habits.

Of course, sometimes the stress or boredom that is on the surface is actually caused by deeper issues. These issues can be tough to think about, but if you're serious about making changes then you have to be honest with yourself.

Are there certain beliefs or reasons that are behind the bad habits? Is there something deeper — a fear, a limiting belief, or an event — that is causing you to hold on to something bad for you?

Recognizing the causes of your bad habits is crucial to replace them.

All of the habits that you have right now — good or bad — are in your life for a reason. In some ways, these behaviors provide a benefit to you, even if they are bad for you in other ways.

In many cases, your bad habit is a simple way to cope with stress. For example, biting your nails, pulling your hair, tapping your foot, or clenching your jaw.

Sometimes the benefit is biological like it is with

smoking. Sometimes it's emotional like it is when you stay in a relationship that is bad for you.

These "benefits" or reasons extend to smaller bad habits as well.

For example, opening your social media page as soon as you turn on your computer might make you feel connected. At the same time looking at all of those emails destroys your productivity, divides your attention, and overwhelms you with stress. But, it prevents you from feeling like you're "missing out" and so you repeat it again.

Because bad habits provide some type of benefit in your life, it's very difficult to simply eliminate them. (This is why simplistic advice like "just stop doing it" rarely works.)

Instead, you need to replace a bad habit with a new habit that provides a similar benefit.

For example, if you smoke when you get stressed, then it's a bad plan to "just stop smoking" when that happens. Instead, you should come up with a different way to deal with stress and insert that new behavior instead of having a cigarette.

In other words, bad habits address certain needs in your life. And for that reason, it's better to replace your bad habits with healthier behavior that addresses that same need. If you expect yourself to simply cut out bad habits without replacing them, then you'll have certain needs that will be unmet and it's going to be hard to stick to a routine of "just don't do it" for very long.

* * *

WHY IT IS CRUCIAL TO ACKNOWLEDGE YOUR BAD HABITS

"The best way to improve your self-control is to see how and why you lose control," Kelly McGonigal

If you're looking for a starting point for replacing bad habits, I'd suggest starting with awareness.

It's easy to get caught up in how you *feel* about your bad habits. You can make yourself feel guilty or spend your time dreaming about how you wish things were ... but these thoughts take you away from what's actually happening.

Instead, it's an awareness that will show you how to actually make real change.

- When does your bad habit actually happen?
- How many times do you do it each day?
- What triggers the behavior and causes it to start?

Simply tracking these issues will make you more aware of the behavior and give you dozens of ideas for stopping it.

Here's a simple way to start tracking your bad habits:

Just track how many times per day your bad habit happens. Each time your bad habit happens, mark it down on your notes app. At the end of the day, count up all of the tally marks and see what your total is.

Your goal isn't to judge yourself or feel guilty about doing something unhealthy or unproductive. The only goal is to be aware of when it happens and how often it happens. Wrap your head around the problem by being aware of it.

Acknowledging bad habits takes a little time and effort, but mostly it takes perseverance. Most people who end up replacing bad habits try and fail multiple times before they make it work. You might not have success right away, but that doesn't mean you can't have it at all.

* * *

HOW TO REPLACE A BAD HABIT WITH A GOOD ONE

"True self-discipline is not when you have someone ordering you to do push-ups, it's when you decide on your own to do them," Stephen Guise

Here are some of the best examples of replacing your bad habits with good ones and thinking about the process in a new way.

You don't need to be someone else, you just need to return to the old you. So often we think that to break bad habits, we need to become an entirely new person. The truth is that you already have it in you to be someone without your bad habits. In fact, it's very unlikely that you had these bad habits all of your life. You don't need to transform into a healthy person, you just need to return to being healthy. You don't need to quit smoking, you just need to return to being a non–smoker. Even if it was years ago, you have already lived without this bad habit, which means you can most definitely do it again.

Use the word "but" to overcome negative self–talk. One thing about battling bad habits is that it's easy to judge yourself for not acting better. Every time you slip up or make a mistake, it's easy to tell yourself how much you suck. Whenever that happens, finish the sentence with "but"...

  - *"I'm out of shape, **but** I could be in shape a few months from now."*
  - *"I'm silly, **but** I'm working to develop a valuable skill."*
  - *"I fell, **but** I am on my way to being better."*

Visualize yourself succeeding. See yourself waking up early or buying healthy food or throwing away cigarettes. Whatever the bad habit is that you are looking to break, visualize yourself crushing it, smiling, and enjoying your success. See yourself building a new identity.

Choose a substitute for your bad habit. You need to have a plan ahead of time for how you will respond when you face the stress or boredom that prompts your bad habit.

- What are you going to do when social media is calling you to procrastinate? (Example: write one sentence for work.)
- What are you going to do when you get the urge to smoke? (Example: deep breathing exercises instead.)

Whatever it is and whatever you're dealing with, you need to have a plan for what you will do instead of your bad habit.

Cut out as many triggers as possible. If the first thing you do when you sit on the sofa is pick up the TV remote, then hide the remote in a different room. If you eat cookies when they are in the house, then throw them all away. If you smoke when you drink, then don't go to the bar. Make it easier on yourself to break bad habits by avoiding the things that cause them.

Surround yourself with people who live the way you want to live. You don't need to ditch your old friends, but don't underestimate the power of finding some new ones.

Join forces with somebody. How often do you try to diet in private? Or maybe you "quit smoking" ... but you kept it to yourself? (That way no one will see you fail, right?) Instead, pair up with someone and quit together. The two of you can hold each other accountable and celebrate your victories together. Knowing that someone else expects you to be better is a powerful motivator.

Plan for failure. We all slip up every now and then. When you screw up, skip a workout, eat bad foods, or sleep in, it doesn't make you a bad person. It makes you human. Recognize your mistakes and move. So rather than beating yourself up over a mistake, plan for it. We all get off track, but what separates top performers from everyone else is that they get back on track very quickly.

* * *

HOW TO LEVERAGE YOUR BEST HABITS

First of all, you should identify habits and activities you know you're good at, and just exploit them as often as you can.

How can you find those exploitative habits? Well, just explore. You do this by spending another percentage of your time asking yourself specific questions that help you determine what comes easy to you but feels like a chore to others. You should constantly be exploring new concepts that you can then exploit for your own gain.

Everyone has at least a few areas in which they could be in the top 10% with some effort. For example, you can write articles and code better than most people.

So start to write and code for 5 minutes a day. Make it your habit and then the magic begins because only a few people can write and code well. It's the combination of the two that makes you so rare.

When you layer habits on top of each other like that, you put yourself in the top one percentile, whereas previously you were in the 20th percentile of any one of those individual skills. And once you're doing something that's both rare *and* valuable, then you have more influence on this world. You become 1 of 100, instead of 1 of 1000. Then it becomes harder to compare you, and your value is more rare in this world.

* * *

THE PRACTICE
OF BUILDING A
NEW HABIT

"We are what we repeatedly do. Excellence, then, is not an act, but a habit," Will Durant

According to researchers at Duke University, habits account for about 40 percent of our behaviors on any given day. Understanding how to build new habits (and how your current ones work) is essential for making progress in your health, your career, and your life in general.

Do you remember the simple formula for building new habits I mentioned in this book? Let's read it again:

Start with a micro-action right now. Repeat it daily. Let it grow with time.

I will guide you to implement this formula into your life to help you build a new habit.

* * *

DAY 1 — START WITH A MICRO-ACTION RIGHT NOW

Start with an incredibly small habit. Make it so easy you can't say no. When most people struggle to build new habits, they say something like, "I just need more time." Or, "I wish I had as much motivation as you do."

This is the wrong approach. Research shows that willpower is like a muscle. It gets fatigued as you use it throughout the day. Another way to think of this is that your motivation ebbs and flows. It rises and falls. You can call it the "motivation wave."

Solve this problem by picking a new habit that is

easy enough that you don't need the motivation to do it.

Rather than trying to meditate for 1 hour per day, start by meditating for one minute right now. Rather than starting with 100 pushups per day, start with 10 pushups right now. Make it easy enough that you can get it done without motivation and just right now.

* * *

DAY 2 — REPEAT

Learning to be patient is perhaps the most critical skill of all. You can make incredible progress if you are consistent and patient. If you are adding weight in the gym, you should probably go slower than you think. If you are adding daily sales calls to your business strategy, you should probably start with fewer than you expect to handle. Patience is everything. Do things you can sustain.

New habits should feel easy, especially in the beginning. If you stay consistent and continue increasing your habit it will get hard enough, fast enough. It always does.

When you slip, get back on track quickly. Even top performers make mistakes, commit errors, and get off track just like everyone else. The difference is that they get back *on track* as quickly as possible.

Research has shown that missing your habit once, no matter when it occurs, has no measurable impact on your long-term progress. Rather than trying to be perfect, abandon your all-or-nothing mentality.

You shouldn't expect to fail, but you should plan for failure. Take some time to consider what will prevent your habit from happening. What are some things that are likely to get in your way? What are some daily emergencies that are likely to pull you off course? How can you plan to work around these issues? Or, at least, how you can bounce back quickly from them and get back on track?

You just need to be consistent, not perfect.

Focus on building the identity of someone who never misses a habit twice.

* * *

DAY 3,4,5,... —
LET IT GROW

Increase your habit in very small ways. Even one percent improvements add up surprisingly fast. So do one percent declines. Rather than trying to do something amazing from the beginning, start small and gradually improve. Along the way, your willpower and motivation will increase, which will make it easier to stick to your habit for good.

If you continue adding one percent each day, then you'll find yourself increasing very quickly within one or two months.

Another good technique to let your new habits grow is to break them into chunks.

Building up to 20 pushups? Split it into two sets of 10 pushups at first.

Trying to meditate for 20 minutes per day? Two segments of 10 minutes might be much easier as you make your way there.

As your habits grow, keep each habit reasonable so that you can maintain momentum and make the behavior as easy as possible to accomplish.

* * *

APPLY MICRO HABITS ELSEWHERE

"Formal education will make you a living, but self-education will make you a fortune," Jim Rohn

Micro Habits is more than just a strategy to teach you how to develop healthy new habits—it's a guide for self-awareness. Use micro habits techniques for any area of your life in which you want to take action. The better you get at micro habits, the more success you'll have in all areas of your life. I wish you a very exciting Micro Habits journey and micro successes, but over and over and over again.

* * *

FINAL NOTE

If you believe this book shares an important message, please leave a review on Amazon. Reviews (in quantity and in rating) are the main metric people use to judge a book's content. And if you have great results with micro habits, please come back and tell other readers (and me) about your success! Every single review has a huge impact on others' willingness to read a book, and if this changes your life, you can change someone else's life by spreading the word.

https://www.amazon.com/dp/B0BVJ2QJ5R

WHAT SHOULD YOU READ NEXT?

Thank you so much for taking the time to read this book. It has been a pleasure sharing my work with you. If you are looking for something to read next, allow me to offer a suggestion. Below you can find a list of book series also written by me and I believe you will find them interesting. This list was updated on February 2023. For the latest updates check my Author Page on Amazon:

https://www.amazon.com/author/kuznietsov_ivan

MICRO HABITS

Microproductivity in 15 Minutes: The Tiny Habit That Will Lead You To Huge Wins

5 STEPS

Sea Soul

The Mountain of Desires

An Epidemic 1,000 Years Before Us

MINDFUL MOMENTS COLLECTION

The Mindful Thrift: How to Appreciate What We Have and Save What We Do Not Notice

The Mindful Nutrition: How to Enjoy the True Taste of Food, Have a Slim Body and 33 (+3) Home Cooking Recipes for a Delicious Degustation

The Mindful Eating for Beginners: Step-by-Step Guide for Lifelong Health and Collection of Quick & Easy Recipes for Every Day

ACKNOWLEDGMENTS

I want to thank my family who supports me on my writing journey. Also, I want to thank all the professionals who helped me publish my work. Finally, I want to thank you, dear reader, for choosing this book from among the millions existing. It's truly inspiring!

NOTES

«Gary A. Klein, Sources of Power: How People Make Decisions (Cambridge, MA: MIT Press, 1998), 38–40.»

«Wood, W., J. M. Quinn, & D. A. Kashy. Habits in everyday life: Thought, emotion, and action. Journal of Personality and Social Psychology. (Dec 2002). v 83(6), 1281-1297.»

«Lally, P., C. H. M. van Jaarsveld, H. W. W. Potts, & J. Wardle. How are habits formed: Modelling habit formation in the real world. Eur. J. Soc. Psychol., (2010). v 40, 998–1009. doi: 10.1002/ejsp.674»